UNICORN

ACTIVITY AND COLOURING BOOK

DREAMLAND PUBLICATIONS
J-128, Kirti Nagar, New Delhi -110 015, India
Tel : +91-11-2510 6050, 2543 5657
E-mail : dreamland@dreamlandpublications.com
Shop online at www.dreamlandpublications.com
Follow us on www.instagram.com/dreamland.publications

Connect the number dots to complete the unicorn. Then colour the picture.

Colour the unicorn in bright shades.

Help the unicorn get his lost shades by copying the colours from the picture below.

Use the grid to copy the drawing, then colour it in.

	1	2	3	4	5	6	7
a							
b							
c							
d							
e							
f							
g							

Find the correct shadow of the unicorn.

Count each object and write its number in the given box.

Find and trace the path of the unicorn to the castle.

Draw a line from each unicorn to its matching shadow.

Let's have some colouring fun with these cute little pictures.

UNICORN
DREAM
Zzzz
LOVE
DREAM

Find the identical pictures.

Help the unicorn to find the right path to the castle.

Mark the differences that you find between the given two pictures.

Colour the unicorn in
beautiful soft shades.

Colour the dancing unicorn in beautiful shades.

Rearrange the letters in the correct order to make a word.

O C U N N I R

Draw a line to match the unicorn that is moving in the same direction.

Hi, it's a sunny day.
Colour me brightly.

Colour the picture brightly.

Match the unicorn to its correct shadow.

Colour the picture using the number key.

1. Dark Pink
2. Light Pink
3. Yellow
4. Magenta
5. Blue
6. Red
7. Aqua

Help the unicorn meet his friend through the maze.

Colour the unicorn using the colours in the number code.

1 2 3 4 5 6

Look at the number given for each picture and solve the given questions.

Find six differences between these two unicorns.

Colour the unicorn with some bright shades.

Colour the picture beautifully.

Use the grid to copy the drawing, then colour it in.

Draw lines to match each picture to the correct silhouette.

Fill in some bright shades in the given picture and dream like a unicorn.

Colour the given picture brightly.

Look at the first picture on each line. Then draw a circle around the pictures that are the same in that row.

Look for and circle the words listed in the column below hidden in the puzzle.

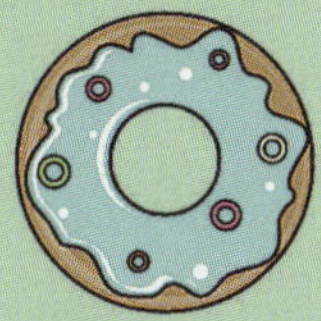

BELIEVE
DREAMS
GLITTER
LOVE
MAGIC
GRACE
UNICORN
WAND
STAR
HEART

G	A	H	E	A	R	T	L
R	D	R	E	A	M	S	O
A	T	D	S	M	K	J	V
C	B	E	L	I	E	V	E
E	U	L	S	H	G	Q	N
O	R	E	M	F	Y	W	S
W	E	W	A	N	D	C	T
I	O	L	G	Z	X	V	A
P	G	L	I	T	T	E	R
U	N	I	C	O	R	N	B

What a beautiful day! Let's enjoy colouring this beautiful picture.

Colour the unicorn below to match the one above.

Find the right path to castles.

There are only two identical unicorns. Find them.

Help the unicorn write the missing numbers and reach the castle.

It's colouring time. Let's colour the unicorn brightly.

Fill in some bright colours in the given picture.

Draw a line to match each picture to its other half.

Count and write how many unicorns are facing to the right and how many are facing to the left.

Left ______ Right ______

Connect the dots to complete the picture. Then colour it in.

Connect the dots 1-58 to complete the picture.
Then colour it in as shown above.

Match the pictures to their correct silhouette.

Draw a path through the maze to help the unicorn reach the doughnut without touching the other objects.

Follow the steps and draw a unicorn.

Colour the given picture.

U is for Unicorn. Colour the given picture brightly.

Use the grid to copy the drawing, then colour it in.

	1	2	3	4	5	6	7
A							
B							
C							
D							
E							
F							
G							

Follow the path pattern and help the unicorn to find the castle.

Look at the value of the objects given below. Then solve the addition sums given above.

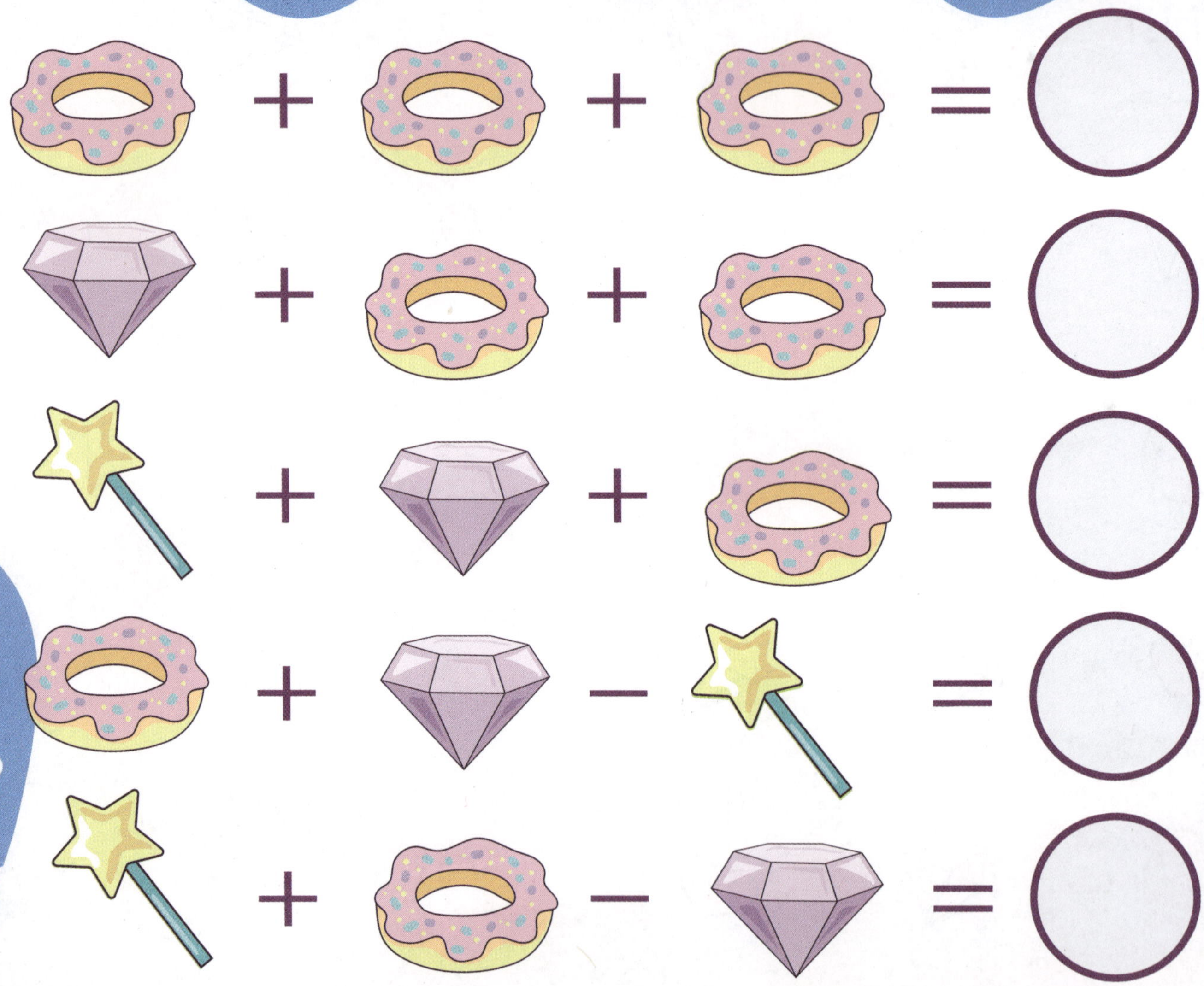